SUPERCARS

# PORSCHE

Ryan Smith

AV2
www.av2books.com

AV2

**Step 1**
Go to **www.av2books.com**

**Step 2**
Enter this unique code
**JGIAKOWZP**

**Step 3**
Explore your interactive eBook!

**AV2 is optimized for use on any device**

# Your interactive eBook comes with...

**Contents**
Browse a live contents page to easily navigate through resources

**Audio**
Listen to sections of the book read aloud

**Videos**
Watch informative video clips

**Weblinks**
Gain additional information for research

**Try This!**
Complete activities and hands-on experiments

**Key Words**
Study vocabulary, and complete a matching word activity

**Quizzes**
Test your knowledge

**Slideshows**
View images and captions

**... and much, much more!**

SUPERCARS

# PORSCHE

## CONTENTS

# POR.

SCHE

# PORSCHE SUPERCARS

Sports cars are meant to be exciting to drive. As sports cars became more powerful, more **luxurious**, and more **exclusive**, they became a new class of car known as a supercar. Supercars are expensive vehicles. They can cost hundreds of thousands or even millions of dollars.

Since 1948, Porsche has built some of the most iconic sports cars in history. Today's Porsche designers are finding new ways to bring the power and luxury of a supercar to everyday driving.

Only **1,270 Porsche Carrera GTs** were ever built.

A **1970 Porsche 917K** sold for more than **$14 million** at auction in **2017**.

# FERRY PORSCHE

***"In the beginning I looked around and could not find quite the car I dreamed of. So I decided to build it myself."*** –Ferry Porsche

Ferdinand Porsche was an **engineer** who built cars. He started the Porsche company in 1931. One of the company's first contracts was to build the VW Beetle for Volkswagen.

Ferdinand's son, Ferdinand Anton Ernst Porsche, was born in 1909. His nanny nicknamed him "Ferry." Ferry started driving when he was 10 years old. His father gave him a special car that was just his size. Ferry took over the Porsche company from his father after **World War II**. He built the company's first sports car, the Porsche 356, in 1948.

The 1,000th Porsche car was built in 1951.

# MAP OF GERMANY

The Porsche factory in Stuttgart, Germany, has been home to Porsche since 1938.

# THE CREST

The Porsche crest was created in 1952. It was meant to show customers that each car had left the factory with the company's **seal** of approval. The Porsche crest was inspired by the coat of arms of the company's home, Stuttgart, and the crest of the former German state of Württemberg-Hohenzollern.

Württemberg-Hohenzollern merged with two other states to form the state of Baden-Württemberg in 1952.

# PORSCHE LOGO

The antlers come from the crest of the state of Württemberg-Hohenzollern.

The Porsche name acts like a protective roof over the rest of the crest.

The red and black colors were the official colors of the state of Württemberg-Hohenzollern.

The black horse comes from the coat of arms of the city of Stuttgart.

# PORSCHE THROUGH HISTORY

**Porsche started out as a company that built cars for other companies. Today, Porsche is known around the world for its luxurious supercars.**

## 1948

Ferry Porsche builds the first car with the Porsche name on it, the Porsche 356.

## 1963

The Porsche 911 is first produced.

## 1972

Ferry's son, Ferdinand Alexander Porsche, founds Porsche Design. The company starts making Porsche watches. Today, Porsche Design makes Porsche accessories including sunglasses and clothing.

Porsche produces its first sport utility vehicle (SUV), the Porsche Cayenne.

## 2002

## 2009

The Porsche Museum opens in the same year as Ferry Porsche's 100th birthday.

## 2019

Porsche unveils its first fully electric car, the Porsche Taycan.

# FAMOUS PORSCHES

One of the most famous collections of Porsche vehicles was in Durham, North Carolina. It was called the Ingram Collection. The collection was owned by businessman Bob Ingram and had more than 80 rare Porsches. It included the third-oldest Porsche 356 in existence. In 2019, a gas pipe explosion damaged the building where the cars were stored. Although many of the cars were out of the building at the time, 20 were destroyed.

Half of the roof of the building that housed the Ingram Collection collapsed in the explosion.

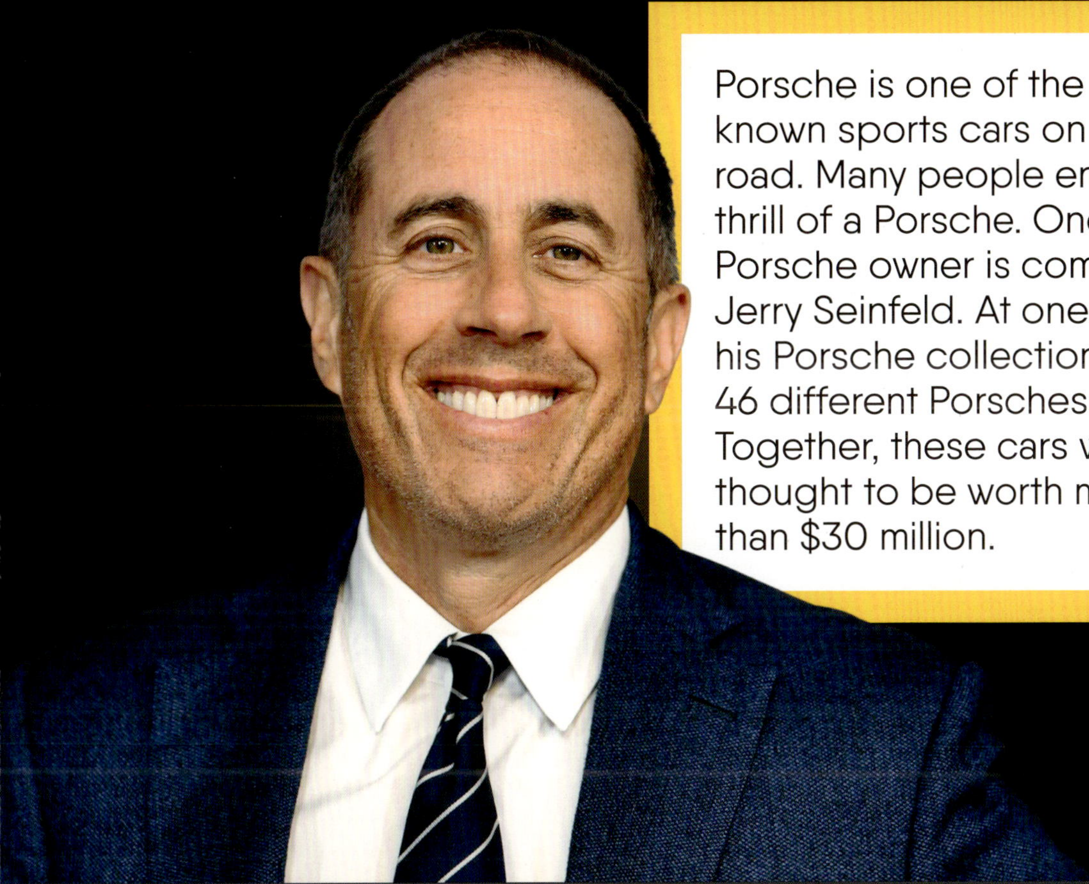

Porsche is one of the best-known sports cars on the road. Many people enjoy the thrill of a Porsche. One famous Porsche owner is comedian Jerry Seinfeld. At one point, his Porsche collection had 46 different Porsches in it. Together, these cars were thought to be worth more than $30 million.

Porsche 911 Carrera

Porsche 550 Spyder

Porsche 917

# AT THE RACES

Porsche takes part in **Grand Touring (GT)** racing. Its GT race team is called GT Works. The team tests new designs and technologies as it races. If the designs do well on the racetrack, they are used in road cars.

At the end of 2019, Porsche entered into **Formula E** racing. The Formula E team races the Porsche 99X Electric. This electric race car can reach speeds up to 174 miles per hour (280 kilometers per hour).

Earl Bamber came in third at the 2019 Macau Grand Prix FIA GT World Cup. He drove a Porsche 911 GT3R.

The 99X Electric can reach 60 mph (100 km/h) in 2.8 seconds.

In **2019**, the **Taycan** set an electric car **lap record** of **7 minutes and 42 seconds** at Germany's Nürburgring racetrack.

The Porsche team finished second and third in the GT Le Mans category of the 2020 Rolex 24 at Daytona endurance race.

**In more than 60 years of racing, Porsche** has **won** more than **30,000** races.

Teams in a GT race have about 30 seconds to change the tires and fill the gas tank.

# HOW IT'S MADE

All of Porsche's sports cars are made in the main factory in Stuttgart. Porsche also builds all of its engines at the main factory. The company opened a second factory in Leipzig, Germany, in 2002. This factory produces the Porsche Panamera **sedan** and the Porsche Macan SUV.

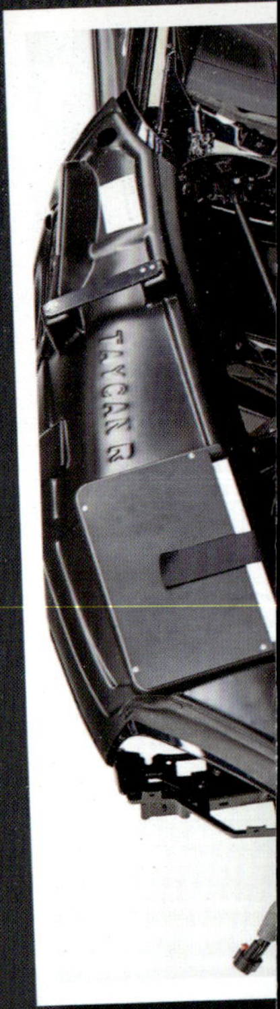

The Porsche Taycan has its own assembly line at the factory.

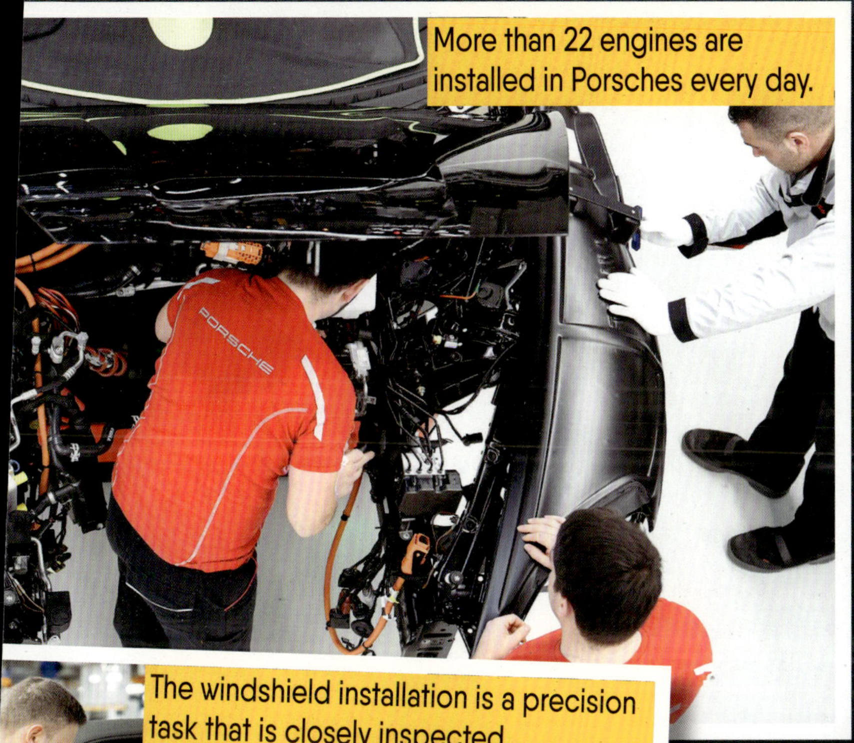


More than 22 engines are installed in Porsches every day.

The **Leipzig factory** produces **160,000 cars a year.**

**Porsche** produced more than **250,000 cars in 2017.**

The windshield installation is a precision task that is closely inspected.

The Porsche crest is one of the last elements to be installed on each car.

# TODAY'S LINEUP

Porsche continues to capture Ferry's love of cars and driving. Today's Porsche **models** provide the thrill of driving a sports car while also meeting the needs of drivers. The Cayenne combines the power of a sports car with the space of an SUV. The Cayenne and the Panamera are also available as **hybrid** cars.

Here are some of the Porsches on the road today.

## Porsche Macan Turbo

Engine: **V6**

Maximum Horsepower: **434**

0–60 mph (0–100 km/h): **4.3 seconds**

Starting Price: **$83,600**

## Porsche 718 Spyder

Engine: **Boxer 6**

Maximum Horsepower: **414**

0–60 mph (0–100 km/h): **4.2 seconds**

Starting Price: **$96,300**

## Porsche Cayenne Turbo S E-Hybrid Coupe

Engine: **V8 and electric motor**

Maximum Horsepower: **670**

0–60 mph (0–100 km/h): **3.6 seconds**

Starting Price: **$164,400**

## Porsche Taycan Turbo S

Engine: **560-kilowatt electric motor**

Maximum Horsepower: **750**

0–60 mph (0–100 km/h): **2.6 seconds**

Starting Price: **$185,000**

## Porsche Panamera Turbo S E-Hybrid Executive

Engine: **V8 and electric motor**

Maximum Horsepower: **677**

0–60 mph (0–100 km/h): **3.3 seconds**

Starting Price: **$198,100**

## Porsche 911 Turbo S Cabriolet

Engine: **Boxer 6**

Maximum Horsepower: **640**

0–60 mph (0–100 km/h): **2.7 seconds**

Starting Price: **$216,300**

# TOMORROW'S PORSCHE

The future of Porsche is electric. In 2015, Porsche began a new project called Mission E. The goal of the project was to create an electric sports car. Mission E's result was the Porsche Taycan. More than 30,000 orders for the Taycan were placed before Porsche began building the **production** version.

Porsche is already looking ahead at building even more powerful electric cars. The Formula E team will test out electric car technologies on the racetrack. As these technologies are perfected, they will be used in Porsche's production electric cars.

Porsche's electric technologies will influence all of its future cars.

The Taycan dashboard is made up of digital screens.

The Formula E team will test technologies such as power boosts and charging while driving.

The Taycan can drive more than 310 miles (500 km) on a single charge.

# PORSCHE QUIZ

**1** How many Porsche Carrera GTs were ever built?

**2** In what year did Ferry build the Porsche 356?

**3** What inspired the Porsche crest?

**4** In what year was the first Porsche 911 produced?

**5** Which comedian had 46 Porsches in his collection at one point?

**6** What car does Porsche race in Formula E?

**7** How many races has Porsche won?

**8** In what year did Porsche open its Leipzig factory?

**9** Which Porsches are available as hybrids?

**10** How many orders were placed for the Porsche Taycan?

**ANSWERS**

**1** 1,270 **2** 1948 **3** The coat of arms of Stuttgart and the crest of Württemberg-Hohenzollernt **4** 1963 **5** Jerry Seinfeld **6** The Porsche 99X Electric **7** More than 30,000 **8** 2002 **9** The Porsche Cayenne and the Porsche Panamera **10** More than 30,000

# KEY WORDS

**engineer:** a person trained in how to build things and use different materials

**exclusive:** limited in number

**Formula E:** single-seat car racing using electric cars

**Grand Touring (GT):** a race car that seats two people

**hybrid:** a car that is powered by both a gas engine and an electric motor

**luxurious:** something that is pleasing, comfortable, and expensive

**models:** the different car designs made by a company

**production:** a type of car design that is meant to be mass produced and sold to the public

**seal:** a symbol used to sign off on something

**sedan:** a car that sits four or more people and has a roof that is fixed in place

**World War II:** a war that was fought from 1939 to 1945

# INDEX

# Get the best of both worlds.

AV2 bridges the gap between print and digital.

The expandable resources toolbar enables quick access to content including **videos**, **audio**, **activities**, **weblinks**, **slideshows**, **quizzes**, and **key words**.

**Animated videos** make static images come alive.

Resource icons on each page help readers to further **explore key concepts**.

Published by AV2
14 Penn Plaza, 9th Floor
New York, NY 10122
Website: www.av2books.com



Library of Congress Cataloging-in-Publication Data

Names: Smith, Ryan, author.
Title: Porsche / Ryan Smith.
Description: New York, NY : AV2, 2020. | Series: Supercars | Includes index. | Audience: Ages 8-12 | Audience: Grades 4-6
Identifiers: LCCN 2020018382 (print) | LCCN 2020018383 (ebook) | ISBN 9781791126001 (library binding) | ISBN 9781791126018 (paperback) | ISBN 9781791126025 | ISBN 9781791126032
Subjects: LCSH: Porsche automobiles--Juvenile literature.
Classification: LCC TL215.P75 S574 2020 (print) | LCC TL215.P75 (ebook) | DDC 629.222--dc23
LC record available at https://lccn.loc.gov/2020018382
LC ebook record available at https://lccn.loc.gov/2020018383

Printed in Guangzhou, China
1 2 3 4 5 6 7 8 9 0 24 23 22 21 20

062020
101119

Art Director: Terry Paulhus Project Coordinator: Ryan Smith



The publisher acknowledges Getty Images and Shutterstock as its primary image suppliers for this title.